Amazing Americans

Thurgood Marshall

Kristin Kemp, M.A.E.

Consultant

Caryn Williams, M.S.Ed.
Madison County Schools
Huntsville, AL

Image Credits: Cover & p.1 Courtesy CSU Archive/
age fotostock; p.9 (bottom) Courtesy Everett Col/
age fotostock; pp.18, 32 AP; p.25 Ron Edmonds/AP;
p.28–29 Becca Spielman; pp.15, 23 (top), 26 Bettmann/
Corbis; p.24 Photo Researchers/Getty Images; pp.5–6,
11, 16 (background) –17 Time & Life Pictures/Getty
Image; p.27 (top) iStock; p.4 LOC [LC-DIG-fsa-8a03228];
p.12–13 LOC [LC-DIG-npcc-32093]; p.12 (top) LOC [LC-
DIG-ppmsca-09709]; p.9 (top) LOC [LC-USZ62-131020];
p.19 LOC [LC-USZ62-112128]; p.20 (left) LOC [LC-
USZ62-60139]; p.13 (top) LOC [na0081p1/The Library
of Congress; pp.8 (right), 14, 16 (top), 21 (right) ZUMA
Press/Newscom; p.22 Dennis Brack/Newscom; p.21 (left)
World History Archive/Newscom; pp. 7 (both), 10, 20
(right) Wikipedia Common; p.31 Yoichi R. Okamoto/U.S.
Government; all other images from Shutterstock.

Library of Congress Cataloging-in-Publication Data

Kemp, Kristin, author.
    Amazing Americans: Thurgood Marshall / Kristin Kemp,
M.A.E.
        pages cm
    Includes index.
    ISBN 978-1-4333-7374-9 (pbk.)
    ISBN 978-1-4807-5160-6 (ebook)
1. Marshall, Thurgood, 1908-1993—Juvenile literature.
2. African American judges—Biography—Juvenile
literature. 3. Judges—United States—Biography—
Juvenile literature. 4. United States. Supreme Court—
Biography—Juvenile literature. 5. African Americans—
Civil rights—History—Juvenile literature. 6. United
States—Race relations—History—Juvenile literature.
I. Marshall, Thurgood, 1908-1993. II. Title.
    KF8745.M34K43 2015
    347.73´2634—dc23
    [B]
                                       2014010605

Teacher Created Materials
5301 Oceanus Drive
Huntington Beach, CA 92649-1030
http://www.tcmpub.com
ISBN 978-1-4333-7374-9
© 2015 Teacher Created Materials, Inc.

Table of Contents

A Man of Change

Thurgood Marshall lived during a time of great unfairness for African Americans. The law said that white people and African Americans could not sit or eat together. They could not use the same swimming pools or restrooms. This was known as "separate but **equal**." The law said African Americans could be separated from white people, as long as what they had was equal, or the same. But Marshall knew things were far from equal. The law was unfair to African Americans, and Marshall spent his life trying to make the law fair for everyone.

Marshall started his career as a **lawyer**. Over time, he became a **judge**. He even became one of the top judges in America. He was a **justice** of the Supreme Court. During his life, Marshall fought for the idea that all people are equal. He worked hard to change unfair laws in America.

COLORED

This African American boy drinks from a separate drinking fountain in 1938.

Thurgood Marshall

Lawyers, Judges, and Justices

Lawyers argue to convince judges that their view of the law is right. Judges decide which lawyer is right or if a law has been broken. Justices are judges on the Supreme Court—the highest court in America.

Growing Up

Marshall was born on July 2, 1908. His family lived in Maryland. Marshall's parents wanted the best for him and his older brother. His father was a waiter, and his mother was a teacher. She wanted Marshall to have a good education.

Marshall went to a segregated school like this one.

Thoroughgood?

Marshall was named Thoroughgood after his great-grandfather. But, Marshall changed his name to Thurgood when he was in second grade. He wanted a shorter name that was easier to spell.

Marshall's high school was **segregated** (SEG-ri-gey-tid). This meant that African Americans and white students were kept apart. Marshall was a good student. But, he got in trouble often. Marshall's principal would make him copy the **U.S. Constitution** (kon-sti-TOO-shuhn) as punishment. This is the main set of laws for America. Marshall was in trouble so often that he ended up memorizing the Constitution! This turned out to be a good thing. Marshall realized that not all of the ideas in the Constitution applied to him. He was not being treated fairly due to the color of his skin. So Marshall decided to be a lawyer. He wanted everyone to have the same rights.

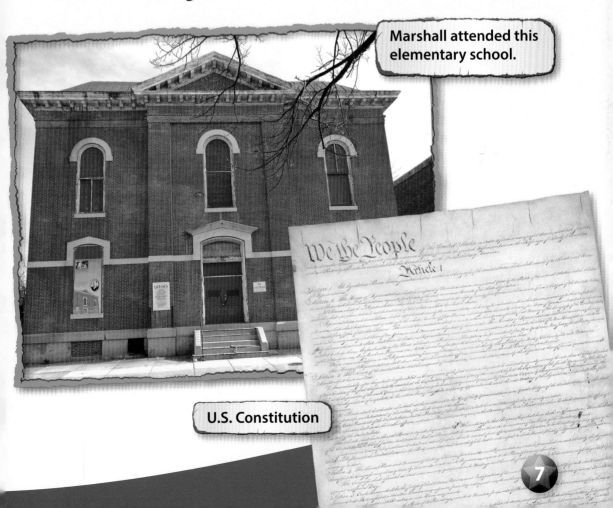

Marshall attended this elementary school.

We the People

Article I

U.S. Constitution

After high school, Marshall went to college. He went to Lincoln University in Pennsylvania (pen-suhl-VEYN-yuh). Marshall's mother wanted him to be a dentist. But Marshall did not want to be a dentist. He liked **debating**. And he wanted to help change unfair laws.

In 1930, Marshall graduated from college. He wanted to go to law school at the University of Maryland. Law school is where people learn to be lawyers and judges. But that school only let white people attend. The fact that he could not go to the school because of the color of his skin hurt Marshall deeply. It had a lasting effect on him.

Buster

Before his last year of college, Marshall married a woman named Vivien Burey (VIV-ee-uhn BUHR-ee). But, everyone called her Buster.

Vivien Burey

Marshall went to Howard University instead. This was a college for African Americans in Washington, DC. Marshall loved learning about the law. He worked very hard and got good grades. His favorite professor was named Charles Houston. The two men were friends for many years. When Marshall graduated in 1933, he was the top student!

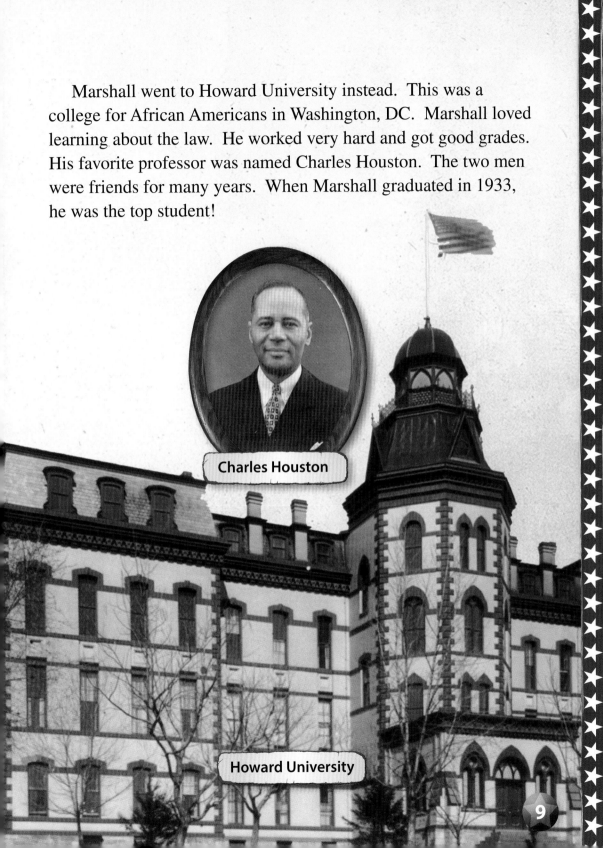

Charles Houston

Howard University

Leading Lawyer

After law school, Marshall went back home to Maryland. There, he started a law practice. This is a business that a group of lawyers run. They **represent** people in court cases.

This was during the Great Depression (dih-PRESH-uhn). Some people wanted to hire Marshall to be their lawyer. But they did not have money to pay him. He often took cases for free. He wanted to help people in need.

Great Depression

The Great Depression was a time in the 1930s when many people did not have jobs. Many people in America were poor and hungry during this time.

This mother and her children struggle during the Great Depression.

Marshall sits at his desk at the NAACP in 1949.

Marshall's friend, Houston, had a new job. He was working for the NAACP. The NAACP fought for the **civil rights** of African Americans. Civil rights are things that all people should have, such as the right to be free.

Houston and the NAACP wanted to get rid of segregation. They wanted all people to live, learn, and work together. They wanted everyone to be treated fairly. Houston asked Marshall to help. Marshall was excited for this chance to help change unfair laws.

University of Maryland

Marshall, Murray, and Houston appear in court in 1935.

One of Marshall's first cases was against the University of Maryland. This was the same school that would not let Marshall attend just five years earlier. In 1935, it still would not accept African Americans. A young man named Donald Murray wanted to go to school there. He was not accepted due to the color of his skin.

All of the law schools in Maryland would only take white students. Some people said that law schools should be separate but equal. But Marshall said that there was no "equal" school for Murray in the state. The "separate but equal" idea would not work.

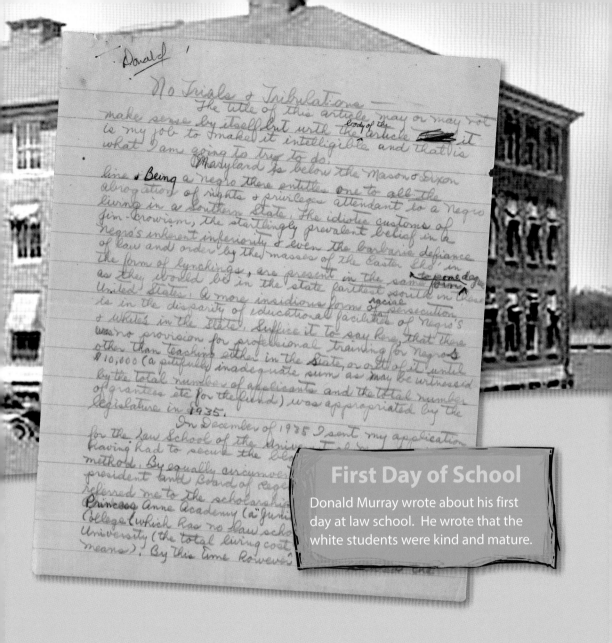

Donald

No Trials & Tribulations

The title of this article may or may not make sense by itself but with the body of the article it is my job to make it intelligible and that is what I am going to try to do.

Maryland is below the Mason & Dixon line & Being a negro there entitles one to all the abrogation of rights & privileges attendant to a Negro living in a Southern State. The idiotic customs of Jim Crowism, the startlingly prevalent belief in a Negro's inherent inferiority & even the barbaric defiance of law and order by the masses of the Easter Sho' in the form of lynchings, are present in the same form as they would be in the state farthest south in the United States. A more insidious form of racial persecution is in the disparity of educational facilities of Negro's & whites in the State. Suffice it to say Rev, that there was no provision for professional training for Negros other than teaching either in the State, or out of it until $10,000 (a pitifully inadequate sum as may be witnessed by the total number of applicants and the total number of grantees etc. for the field) was appropriated by the legislature in 1935.

In December of 1935 I sent my application for the Law School of the University... having had to secure the ... method. By equally circumvent... president & Board of Rege... referred me to the scholarship... Princess Anne Academy (a "juni... College (which has no law sch... University (the total living cost... means). By this time Rowev's...

First Day of School

Donald Murray wrote about his first day at law school. He wrote that the white students were kind and mature.

The school's lawyer said that Maryland had a **scholarship** (SKOL-er-ship) for African Americans. This means that they could use the money to go to a school in another state. The judge agreed with Marshall that this was not good enough. Marshall won the case! Murray was able to go to the University of Maryland.

Later in 1936, Marshall was asked to be the NAACP's top lawyer. He moved to New York City. He worked on many cases. He helped African Americans who were treated unfairly. In court, Marshall was a good storyteller and very likable. He was also great at debating. These qualities helped make him a strong lawyer.

Most of Marshall's cases were about segregation in schools. So, the Supreme Court joined all these cases into one big case. Marshall wanted to get rid of the idea of "separate but equal." He argued that there was no such thing. He believed that people would never feel equal if they were segregated.

The case is known as *Brown v. Board of Education*. Marshall knew that winning this case would change America. In 1954, the Supreme Court reached a **verdict**. It said that "separate but equal" for schools was against the law. Marshall won!

Marshall celebrates after winning the *Brown v. Board of Education* case in 1954.

What Do You Mean by Equal?

During the case, Marshall was asked by a justice what he meant by the word equal. Marshall said, "Equal means getting the same thing, at the same time, and in the same place."

A mother explains the *Brown v. Board of Education* case to her daughter.

The News

HIGH COURT BANS SEGREGATION IN PUBLIC SCHOOLS

Rosa Parks is arrested in 1955.

The *Brown v. Board of Education* case was a big win for Marshall. His next goal was to end segregation everywhere, not just in schools. A woman named Rosa Parks gave him his chance.

In 1955, buses in Alabama were segregated. The law in Alabama said that only white people could sit in the front of the bus. African Americans had to sit in the back of the bus. And if there were not enough seats for everyone, then African Americans needed to stand up so that white people could sit down.

One day, Parks refused to give up her seat for a white man. The police arrested her. Her case went to the Supreme Court. Marshall was her lawyer. He said that all segregation should be **illegal** (ih-LEE-guhl), or against the law. The Supreme Court agreed. It was another important win for African American civil rights.

Sad News

While Marshall was working on the Rosa Parks case, he received some sad news. His wife, Buster, was very sick. He took time off work to take care of her, but she passed away. Later, Marshall would marry a woman named Cecilia Suyat (suh-SEEL-ee-uh soo-YAHT). Her nickname was Cissy.

Cissy and Marshall

17

Taking a Break

By 1960, Marshall had been working for the NAACP for more than 20 years. He had helped end some segregation laws in America. He had inspired many African Americans to keep fighting for their civil rights.

But many white people did not want segregation to end. They were mad at Marshall. They sent him angry letters and said that they would hurt him if he kept working for equality. Even some civil rights leaders did not like Marshall. They felt that changing laws took too long. They wanted to make changes with **boycotts** (BOI-kotz) and protests. Marshall needed to take a break.

People protest in Alabama.

Marshall and Kenya leader, Jomo Kenyatta (JOH-moh ken-YAH-tuh)

Marshall traveled to Kenya in Africa. This country belonged to Great Britain, but it wanted to be free like the United States. Marshall spent time with the leaders in Kenya. He helped them write a constitution for their new government. After he helped them, the new leaders gave him a coat. Marshall kept the coat for the rest of his life.

New Roles

When Marshall returned to the United States, he was ready for a new challenge. President John F. Kennedy had one for him. Marshall had been a very good lawyer. The president thought that he would be a good judge, too. In 1961, Kennedy chose Marshall to be a judge on the Court of Appeals. This court is where people go if they do not agree with the verdict of their case. Marshall got to make the final decisions on many cases. Some cases were about civil rights. Other cases were about business.

President
John F. Kennedy

Thurgood Marshall

In 1963, there was a new president. And there was a new job for Marshall. President Lyndon B. Johnson asked him to be **Solicitor** (suh-LIS-i-ter) **General**. Marshall would now represent the government in court. He argued many cases before the Supreme Court.

Marshall was only the second African American to be a judge in the Court of Appeals. And he was the first to be Solicitor General!

Civil Rights Act

In 1964, President Johnson approved the Civil Rights Act. This law said that people could not be treated differently because of their skin color. It made segregation illegal in the United States.

President Lyndon B. Johnson signs the Civil Rights Act.

By 1967, President Johnson thought that Marshall was doing a great job. But the president wanted Marshall to have an even higher position. The Supreme Court had never had an African American justice before. The president knew that Marshall would be perfect for the job. Johnson said, "It was the right thing to do, the right time to do it, the right man, and the right place." Marshall knew a lot about the Supreme Court. He had been debating cases there for years. Now, he would be making decisions for the Supreme Court.

While Marshall was a justice, he kept working for civil rights. He wanted rights for women. And he thought that American Indians' rights were important, too. He also wanted to protect the poor.

Marshall did not always agree with the other justices of the Supreme Court. But he always did what he thought was right for America.

Marshall and President Johnson

Cissy fixes Marshall's robe before he is sworn in as a Supreme Court Justice.

Time to Resign

Justices can serve on the Supreme Court for as long as they want. Marshall always thought that he would be a justice for the rest of his life. But after almost 24 years, his health was failing. His heart was weak and he could not see very well. He was 82 years old.

Marshall decided that it was time to stop working. He **resigned** (ri-ZAHYND) from the Supreme Court in 1991. A reporter asked Marshall why he was leaving. He joked, "I'm getting old and coming apart!" Many people were surprised by Marshall's decision to leave the court. His fellow justices were sad to see him resign.

Thurgood Marshall enjoyed his time as a Supreme Court justice.

On January 24, 1993, Marshall passed away. His body was brought to the Supreme Court building where thousands of people came to honor him. His funeral was shown on television. Many people spoke about the ways that he helped African Americans. Americans knew that they had lost a true hero.

Marshall's body is viewed in the Supreme Court building.

Mr. Civil Rights

People have done many things to honor Marshall. The University of Maryland's law school named its library after him. This is the same school that would not let him attend due to the color of his skin. There is also a statue of Marshall in his hometown. It stands in front of the courthouse. His picture was put on a U.S. postage stamp. There is even a college named after him!

Marshall's nickname was "Mr. Civil Rights." He used the law to fight for civil rights. Marshall did not believe in "separate but equal." He spent his life working to end segregation. He fought hard for equality.

Thurgood Marshall was a lawyer, a judge, and a Supreme Court justice. No matter which job he had, he always tried to make the United States a better and more fair place.

Marshall sits outside the Supreme Court in 1979.

statue of Marshall in his hometown, Baltimore, Maryland

Thurgood Marshall U.S. postage stamp

Amazing Americans Today

Thurgood Marshall was an amazing American. He helped people by fighting for civil rights and making sure everyone was treated equally.

Becca's amazing American is her grandmother Annette. She loves to help people in her community by cooking and sharing meals with them. She also teaches table manners to kids. She believes that making food is an important skill for kids to learn.

Ask It!

Ask an adult to help you find an amazing American in your community. Interview that person. Find out what he or she does to make your community a better place.

An amazing American I know is my grandma. She is an amazing American. Because she cooks and gives food to people who need it.

Pasta

salad

Picture of grammy

This is a picture Becca drew of her grandmother cooking.

Glossary

boycotts—when people refuse to buy, use, or participate in something as a way of protesting

civil rights—rights that every person should have

debating—discussing something with people whose opinions are different from your own

equal—the same

illegal—against the law

judge—a person who has the power to make decisions on cases brought before a court of law

justice—a judge in the Supreme Court

lawyer—a person whose job is to guide and assist people in matters relating to the law

represent—speak or act for someone or something officially

resigned—gave up a job in a formal and official way

scholarship—an amount of money that is given to a student to help pay for his or her education

segregated—to separate groups of people because of their race or religion

Solicitor General—someone who represents the government in court

U.S. Constitution—the system of beliefs and laws by which the United States is organized

verdict—the decision made by a judge or jury in a trial

Index

Your Turn!

Be Fair!

Think about your community. Is there something that you feel is not fair? Is there a law or rule that does not treat everyone equally? Write a letter to a community leader explaining how you think things could be more fair.